DRAW
ANIMALS!

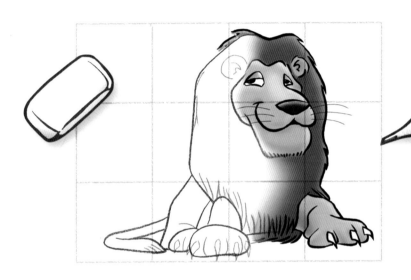

Damien Toll

MUD PUDDLE BOOKS, INC.
New York, New York

Draw Animals!

Written & Illustrated by
Damien Toll

Published by
Mud Puddle Books, Inc.
54 W. 21st Street
Suite 601
New York, NY 10010

info@mudpuddlebooks.com

ISBN: 978-1-60311-034-1

Originally published as
You Can Draw Wild Animals
and You Can Draw Sea Creatures
by Hinkler Books Pty Ltd
17-23 Redwood Drive
Dingley Victoria 3172 Australia

www.hinklerbooks.com

Printed and bound in China

Contents

Introduction

Drawing is a fun and rewarding hobby for children and adults alike. This book is designed to show how easy it is to draw great pictures by building them in simple stages.

What you will need.

Only basic materials are required for effective drawing. These are:

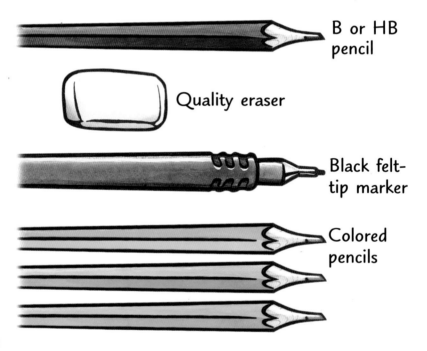

B or HB pencil

Quality eraser

Black felt-tip marker

Colored pencils

These will be enough to get started. Avoid buying the cheapest pencils. Their leads often break off in the sharpener, even before they can be used. The leads are also generally too hard, making them difficult to see on the page.

Cheap erasers also cause problems by smudging rather than erasing. This often leaves a permanent stain on the paper. By spending a little more on art supplies in these areas, problems such as these can be avoided.

When purchasing a black marker, choose one to suit the size of your drawings. If you draw on a large scale, a thick felt-tip marker may be necessary. If you draw on a medium scale, a medium-point marker will do and if on a small scale, a 0.3mm, 0.5mm, 0.7mm or 0.8mm felt-tip marker will best suit.

The Stages

Simply follow the lines drawn in orange on each stage using your B or HB pencil. The blue lines on each stage show what has already been drawn in the previous stages.

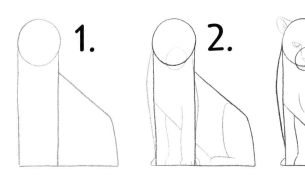

In the final stage the drawing has been outlined in black and the simple shape and wire-frame lines erased. The shapes are only there to help us build the picture. We finish the picture by drawing over the parts we need to make it look like our subject with the black marker, and then erasing all the simple shape lines.

Included here is a sketch of the leopard as it would be originally drawn by an artist.

These are how all the animals in this book were originally worked out and drawn. The orange and blue stages you see above are just a simplified version of this process. The drawing here has been made by many quick pencil strokes working over each other to make the line curve smoothly. It does not matter how messy it is as long as the artist knows the general direction of the line to follow with the black marker at the end. The pencil lines are erased and a clean outline is left. Therefore, do not be afraid to make a little mess with your B or HB pencil, as long as you do not press so hard that you cannot erase it afterwards.

Grids made of squares are set behind each stage in this book. Make sure to draw a grid lightly on your page so it does not press into the paper and show up after being erased. Artist tips have also been added to show you some simple things that can make your drawing look great. Have fun!

The Elephant

The elephant is the largest land mammal in the world. This huge animal can weigh more than four and a half tons and can spend up to 20 hours a day eating grass, leaves and bark. Elephants live in groups called herds. An elephant's life span can be as long as 80 years.

1.

Draw a grid with four equal squares going across and three down.

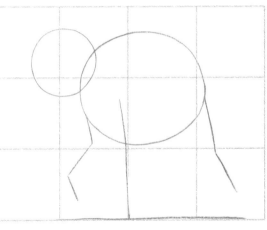

Draw the oval for the body first. Next draw the circle for the head. Notice how the front wire-frame leg is at the end of the body shape. The middle wire-frame is nearly half way along the body shape. The last wire-frame leg is at the other end of the body shape.

Draw in a ground line and check everything is in the right position.

2.

Draw in the tusk near the bottom left of the head circle. Add on the legs based on the wire-frames. Notice how the middle leg extends right up into the body.

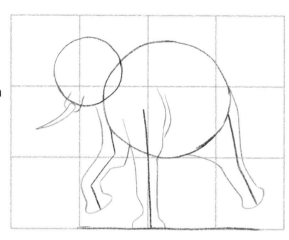

The back leg flows smoothly onto the body shape so there is no way to tell where it joins.

3.

The trunk flows off the head at the front in the same way the back leg flowed off the body shape in the previous stage.

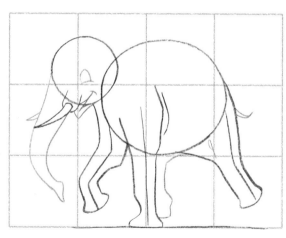

The mouth starts under the tusk and extends outside the head circle. Above the mouth is the cheek and eye.

Add in the other back leg, which is situated behind the middle leg. Draw in the crease in the back leg and add on the tail.

4.

Draw on the curved ridges of the trunk. Add the eyeball and the ears.

Imagine where the front of the elephant's foot is on each leg and add some toenails.

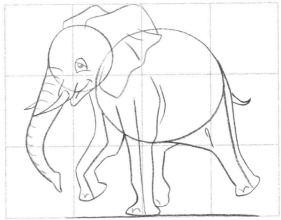

When you are ready to outline your artwork remember to only draw in the lines needed to make the picture. Check the final picture to see which ones you need.

5.

Once you have rubbed out the pencil lines, color your elephant and add some dry grass.

The Lion

Lions live and hunt in groups called prides. Great eyesight and a keen sense of smell help the lion catch its prey. When chasing, they can reach speeds of up to 50 mph (80 kph). Resting is also important. A lion can sleep for up to 20 hours a day. A lion's roar can be heard more than 3 miles (5 km) away. Only male lions have a mane.

1.

Draw a grid with four equal squares going across and three down.

Start by drawing a shape for the snout. Add a similar shape for the head behind it. Check to see if your drawing is correctly positioned on the grid.

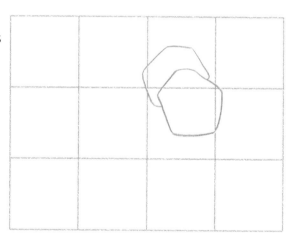

2.

Draw in another shape around the first two shapes. This will be the mane around the neck.

Add shapes for the feet and the legs coming out of the mane.

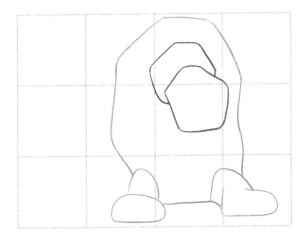

3.

Draw in the shapes for the back leg, foot and tail.

Draw in the nose on the right side of the snout shape. Modify the mane that was drawn in the last stage.

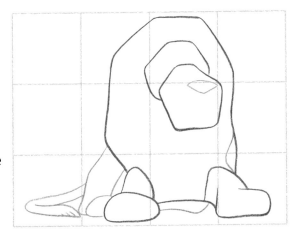

4.

Draw in some lines and points to make the mane look scruffy.

Put the ears on just outside of the head shape. Draw the eyes pushed up by the cheeks. Divide the mouth parts into a curved "W" and define the bottom jaw.

Finally, divide the foot into paws and add sharp nails.

5.

Outline your lion with a felt-tip marker and rub out the pencil lines. You are now ready to color. Keep the body a tan color while making the mane a darker, more reddish color.

Hippopotamus

The hippopotamus is a huge animal that can grow to be over 13 feet (4 m) long and weigh nearly two tons. Its head alone can weigh a ton. It eats up to 100 lbs (45 kgs) of leaves per night and during the day retreats to the cool of the river where it can drink up to 66 gals (250 liters) of water. Hippos are only found in Africa where they live in herds.

1.

Draw a grid with four equal squares going across and three down.

Draw in the head circle first. Add the body shape. Make sure the body shape is correct before going to the next stage.

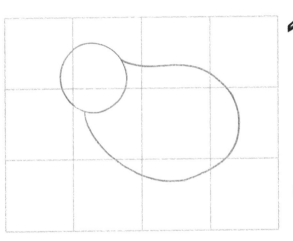

2.

Draw in a wobbly line for a water line. The water line in front of the hippo should be a little lower than the rest of the water line.

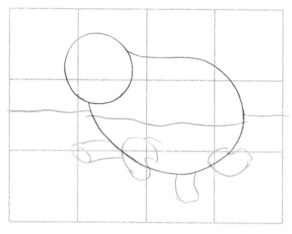

Note where the legs are in relation to the grid and draw them in. Because the legs are so short there is no need for wire-frames here.

3.

Draw the mouth and define the eye on the head circle.

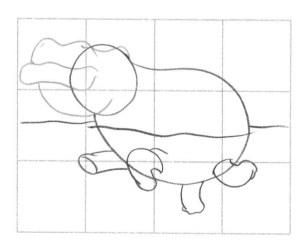

4.

Add on the eye and ear and the creases on the back of the neck, and you are ready to outline your hippo.

5.

Color your hippo and the water. Notice how the hippo is darker below the water line.

Rhinoceros

Rhinos are large animals found in both Africa and Asia. They can grow to be nearly six feet (2 m) tall, 12 feet (4 m) long and weigh almost two and a half tons. Being herbivores, they only eat grass and leaves and sometimes plants with sharp thistles. Rhinos have excellent hearing but cannot see things close to them very well.

1.

Draw a grid with four equal squares going across and three down.

Start with an oval for the head. This oval is on a slight angle. Draw in two larger and wider shapes behind the first oval. Notice these shapes are pointier than a normal oval. They are more like an egg on top.

Check that your shapes are correct and in the right places on the grid.

2.

Use the grid to position the horns on the head circle. Draw in the lip outside the head circle.

The eye is slightly below the center of one of the grid squares. Draw a leaf shape for the ear in the top half of the grid square.

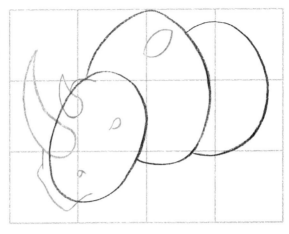

3.

Draw in the other ear opposite the first ear. Continue the head above the first head circle. Add some crease lines around the first ear and around the eye.

Draw in the legs and rounded shapes for the feet.

4.

Draw creases in the shoulder above the front leg. Draw a curved line between the front and back leg to define the stomach.

Break the feet up into toes. Notice how the back toes are smaller than the front ones.

5.

Outline your rhino and erase the pencil lines. Rhinos can be different colors, from white to grey to brown. You could put a shadow just below the rhino's feet to show it is in the air running.

The Cheetah

Cheetahs are long, thin cats and are well designed for speed. In a chase, they reach speeds in excess of 60 mph (100 kph). This makes them the fastest animal in the world. Cheetahs cannot roar, but make a sound called a "chirrup".

1.

Draw a grid with two equal squares going across and four down.

Draw in the basic shapes in the correct position on the grid. Check to make sure your shapes look the same as the shapes on our grid.

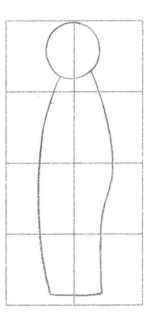

2.

Add another circle in the lower left corner of the original circle. This is for the snout. Draw the ears on the head circle.

Add shapes for the back legs on either side of the long body shape. Draw the two long lines inside the body shape. These will make up the front legs. Finally, add in the shapes for the feet.

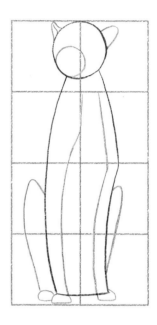

3.

Put the nose on the small circle drawn in the second stage. Position it just left of the center of the bottom circle. Now break up the circle by drawing the curved "W" shape that makes up the cheeks and bottom jaw. Draw the whiskers coming out from each side of the cheeks.

Draw in the eyes, taking notice where they are positioned on the head circle. They are over half way up the circle and on the left hand side of it.

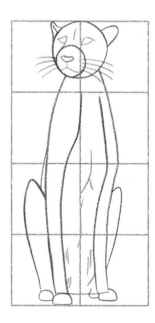

Draw in the line for the cheetah's back next to the leg on the left and some lines for the chest half way down the cheetah. Add some lines to show fur. Finish with the shape for the back foot on the right.

4.

Add spots to the legs, back and head. Notice how the spots fade out by getting smaller around the face and eventually stop.

Be careful not to put spots too far into the chest or on the snout. Color your cheetah using yellow for the base and orange for the back, legs and head. Leave the snout and the chest lighter than the rest of the animal.

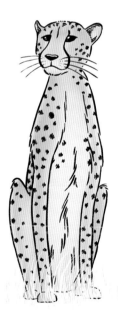

The Leopard

Leopards are very strong and fast members of the cat family. They can drag freshly-caught animals that are much heavier than themselves up a tree to keep them away from lions and hyenas. They are amazing jumpers, able to leap 20 feet (6 meters) forward in a single bound and 10 feet (3 meters) straight up. Each leopard has its own unique spot pattern.

1.

Draw a grid with three equal squares going across and three down.

First, draw in the head in the top left of the grid. Draw in the tall rectangle on its side under the head circle. Draw in the last shape on the right side to complete this stage.

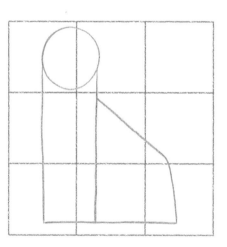

2.

Draw a small circle on the bottom of the head circle just going outside of the head circle.

Draw in the legs around and inside the long rectangle. Draw in the underside of the belly line and add the shapes for the back leg and the foot.

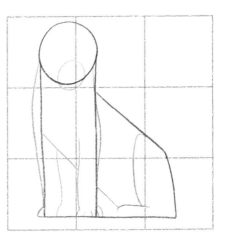

3.

Add the ears to the outside of the head circle. Draw in the facial features, being careful to put them in the correct place on the circles.

Draw in a line to divide the chest. Add the tail and rear foot to finish.

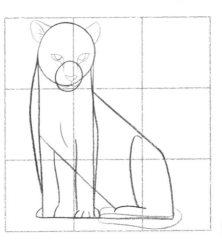

Artist Tip:

The leopard's mouth, chest and stomach are all white. Notice though there is no edge to where the white starts and the coat color finishes. It is a gradual color fade. When coloring with pencil, push harder at the edge of the picture and gradually lighten pressure as you move towards the center of the drawing. You may need to do this a number of times to build up the coat color.

4.

Add spots to the head and chest, making them smaller as they fade out. The spots on the back have holes in them where the color of the coat is slightly darker than the rest of the yellow coat.

Giraffe

At 16 feet (5 m) tall, the giraffe is the tallest animal in the world. It feeds on leaves and can consume 130 lbs (60 kgs) of leaves in one day. The giraffe's heart is as big as a basketball and, if challenged, it can kill a lion using its bony head.

1.

Draw a grid with three equal squares going across and four down.

First, draw in the shape for the body on the grid. Draw the pointy head shape and connect it to the body with a wire-frame.

Add in the curved and kinked wire-frames for the legs. Lastly, draw in a ground line.

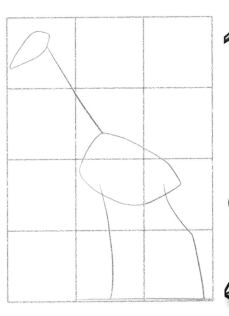

2.

Draw in the horn on the head and the facial features. Add the neck, being sure to make it slightly wider as it goes down towards the body.

Draw in the legs around the wire-frame guides and add the new wire-frames for the legs behind. Add on the tail.

3.

Add the other horn on the head, and the far legs. Draw the mane on the back of the neck. Giraffes' manes are fairly short so don't make it too thick.

Finally, add in the shapes for the pattern on the coat. Notice how they get smaller and fade out on the face and legs.

4.

Add spots all over the legs, back and head. Be careful not to put spots too far into the chest or on the snout. Color your picture.

The Meerkat

Found in South Africa, the meerkat is a social animal. They love to play while one keeps watch for predators. During the day meerkats hunt for food. They eat worms, lizards, insects and fruit. At night the meerkat sleeps in a burrow.

1.

Draw a grid with two equal squares going across and four down.

Draw in the basic shapes for the body and head in the correct position on the grid. Check to make sure your shapes look the same as the shapes on our grid.

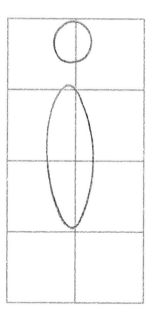

2.

Draw the little ear on the head circle. Draw the neck and arms with rounded shapes for the paws.

Complete this stage by drawing in the legs and feet. Notice how one leg looks almost straight but the other one is kinked. The leg that is straight is facing towards us, while the other one is turned to the side.

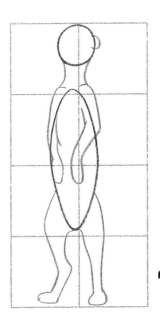

3.

Add the snout onto the head circle with the nose, chin and eye. Divide the chest and stomach with two vertical lines. Separate the rounded paws into fingers. Draw in the tail and you are ready to outline.

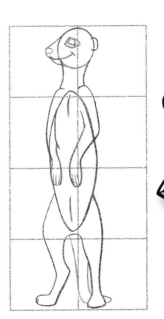

4.

Meerkats range from being light yellow to dark orange. They are greyish white on their belly. They also have a dark patch around their eye and on the end of their tails.

The Fox

The Red Fox is the biggest in the fox family. They are slightly bigger than a cat and have a big, bushy tail. Foxes live around the edges of forests in England and hunt alone at night. They eat rabbits, mice, birds and sometimes worms and beetles. The fox is at the top of its food chain and has no predators. Foxes are often thought of as being very clever.

1.

Draw a square grid with three equal squares going across and down.

Start with a circle near the top left of the grid. Draw another slightly warped oval shape under the circle. Check your shape with this shape to make sure they look the same.

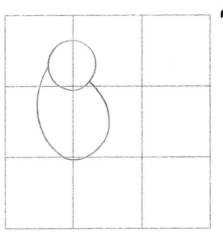

2.

Add on the ears to the outside of the first shape.

Draw another shape to the right of the warped oval to form the back of the animal. Draw in the wire-frame lines for the legs, paying close attention to putting them in the right position.

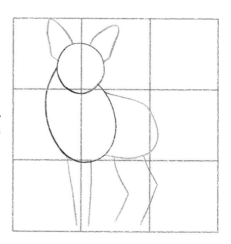

3.

Draw the shape of the legs around the wire-frames, using the wire-frames as a guide to keep them straight.

4.

Add in the cheek fur on the outside of the original circle. Then draw in the facial features on the bottom right of the circle. Add the bushy tail.

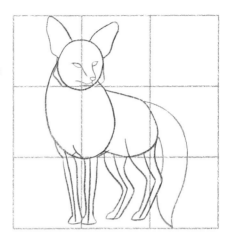

5.

Outline only those shapes you need to make the fox, rub out the guide lines and color the fox to your heart's content.

Red Squirrel

The Red Squirrel lives in trees. It can be found in America, Canada and England. They are excellent climbers and can leap from branch to branch around the forest canopy. Squirrels are wary creatures. Great eyesight, sense of smell and hearing all help to protect the squirrel from predators. A squirrel can fall from great heights out of a tree and live.

1.

Draw a grid with three equal squares going across and down.

Start by drawing in a circle for the body shape a little lower than the middle of the grid.

Draw in the head shape, which looks like an egg facing towards the ground on an angle.

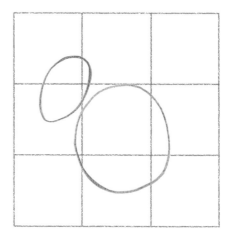

2.

Connect the head shape to the body shape with a curved line.

Draw on the arms. Notice how the arms flow off the edge of the circle at the top.

The squarish shape for the back legs also flows off the body at the back. Check your drawing is correct and move onto the next stage.

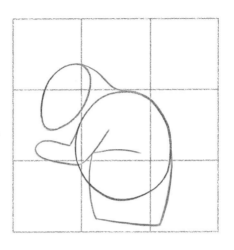

3.

Here we have drawn in the ears. They are curved to a point at the top. Draw on a little shape for the nose and add the other paw beside the first arm.

Draw in the other leg at the front. Draw in the long, thick tail that curves around the body and extends above the head and ears.

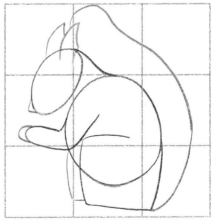

4.

Draw in an oval shape for the nut in its paws. Draw in a curved line that goes from the top of the nut to the body circle for its neck. Add in the other arm below the neck.

Draw the claws on the feet at the base of the square shapes for the legs.

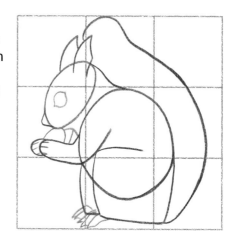

5.

Outline your squirrel and erase the pencil lines. Color it with red while using brown for the shaded areas.

Weasel

Weasels can be found in the forests of America, Canada and England. The weasel is best known for its ability to get through very small holes and crevices. They can also climb trees very easily. They will hunt rabbits, mice, snakes, moles and even eat insects. Preferring to hunt at night, the weasel will search out the tunnels made by these animals for its next meal.

1.

Draw a grid with four equal squares going across and two down.

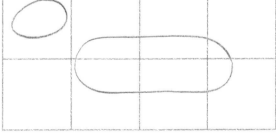

Begin with a shape that looks like a short sausage for the body. Check it is in the correct position on your grid.

Draw a shape like an egg pointing forward in the top left corner of the grid.

2.

Extend a point on the end of the head circle and curve it back under the chin. Add an eye in the head circle.

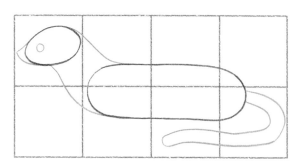

Draw a flowing line from the bottom of the head circle to the body shape. Do the same for the top.

Add a long, curved tail onto the sausage shape.

3.

Draw in some ears on the head shape. One is poking out the top and the other one is crossing over the head shape into the neck.

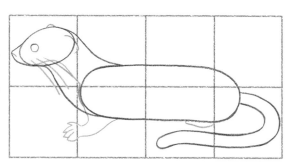

Draw in a few whiskers and a small line for the nose. Draw a line from the chin to the sausage shape.

Add the front leg and a little shape for the back leg.

Artist Tip:

Making something look furry only takes a few carefully positioned pen strokes. The pen strokes come off the outline only slightly and a new line is begun underneath. Drawing too many strokes for hair darkens and unbalances the picture.

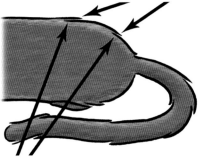

Stroke end comes off shape

New stroke begins under previous stroke

4.

Color your weasel a reddish brown, leaving the chest white. Color the eye black, leaving a white highlight at the top of it.

Platypus

Platypus are only found on the east coast of Australia. They are about half the size of a house cat. They have a bill like a duck and a tail like a beaver. They use their bill to forage for food along the bottoms of rivers. They eat fish, fish eggs, frogs and tadpoles. A platypus is able to hold its breath for ten minutes under water. At night they sleep in burrows in the river bank.

1.

Draw a grid with four equal squares going across and two down.

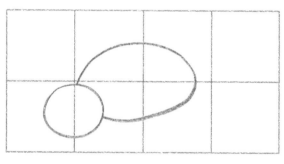

Begin with a circle in the bottom left of the grid. Add a shape for the body. Notice how the body shape is slightly rounder on top than on its underside. Check that you have drawn the body shape correctly and move onto stage two.

2.

Here we add the bill. It is very wide and fairly flat.

Add another shape onto the body shape at the rear.

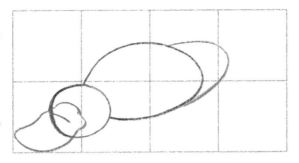

3.

Draw on the arms and legs. When drawing the tail, notice how it is fairly straight and broad.

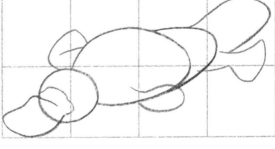

Make sure everything is in the correct position and move onto the next stage.

4.

Here we can finish with the detail. Put a couple of short lines on the end of the bill for the nostrils. Draw the eyes touching the bill.

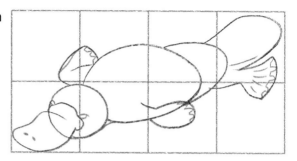

Connect the head circle to the body circle. Break up the shapes on the end of the arms and legs into claws.

5.

Outline your platypus with a felt-tip marker and color it. The platypus here is swimming, so you may like to put some water around it.

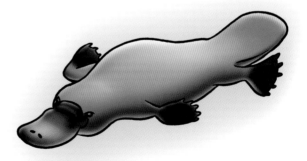

Kangaroo

Kangaroos live in Australia.
They have strong, muscular legs and a thick,
heavy tail. A kangaroo can only move its
back legs together and uses its tail as a third
leg when moving slowly. Kangaroos have
good eyesight and excellent hearing.

1.

Draw a grid with three
equal squares going across
and four down.

First, draw in the body
shape on your grid. Draw
the head next and connect
it to the body shape with a
wire-frame. Check to see
whether your shapes are
positioned correctly on
your grid.

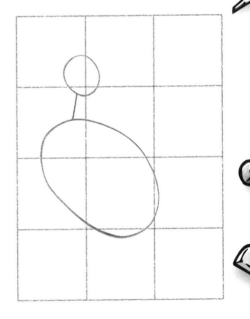

2.

Draw leaf-shaped ears on the head circle. Notice how the ear on the right is slightly smaller because it is further away.

Add the snout and mouth. Draw in the legs and the feet.

3.

The facial features are next with the eye, nostril and dividing line for the cheeks.

Next, draw in the neck and arms. Draw in the underside and the tail to complete this stage.

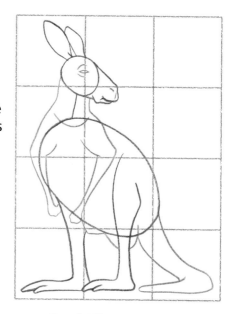

4.

This is an eastern grey kangaroo, so we have colored it a bluish grey.

Crocodile

Crocodiles are large reptiles. They live on both land and water. On land they can move at speeds of 50 mph (80 kph) in short bursts. Under the water they can hold their breath for five hours. They can also go months without eating. Crocodiles are cold-blooded, which means they have to lie in the sun to warm themselves up.

1.

Draw a grid with four equal squares going across and two down.

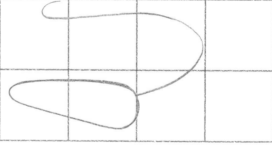

Start with a shape that looks like a stretched egg in the bottom left hand corner of the grid.

Draw in the "S" shaped line. This line is a guide that runs through about the middle of the animal. By having this guide, the body and tail can run in line with it.

2.

Build the body shape along the line, bringing it to a point at the end of the line. Notice how the body widens and then tapers off to a point at the end of the tail.

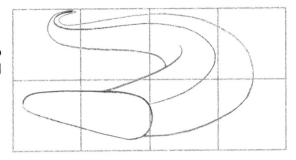

3.

Add the shapes for the legs, being careful to place them in the correct positions on the grid.

Draw in two wavy lines for the croc-odile's mouth.

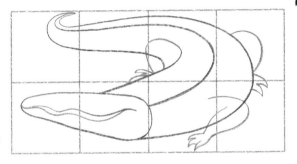

4.

Put in some large, spikey teeth and then add in the rest of the teeth with a simple zig-zag pattern.

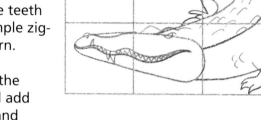

Redefine the snout and add the eyes and edges above the eyes.

Draw in some scales running along the top of the back and then some on the side of the body.

5.

Crocodiles are light colored on their belly and generally a darker green on top.

You may like to draw a river scene in the back-ground. You could draw a set of eyes poking out of the river as if another crocodile is lurking nearby.

The Shark

Sharks are fish. There are over 300 varieties of shark. Some are only a few inches long and some grow to be over 18 feet (6 m) long. The smaller sharks eat plankton while the bigger sharks eat fish, squid, octopuses and seals. Sharks do not have bones, but a skeleton made out of cartilage.

1.

Draw a grid with four equal squares going across and three down.

Draw a pointy egg in the left half of the grid. Notice the angle this egg shape is on.

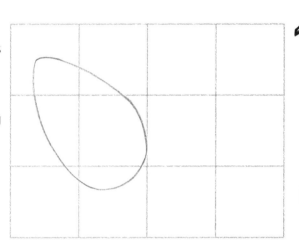

2.

Add a large fin to- wards the bottom of the egg shape reaching down to the lower left cor- ner of the grid.

Draw a hook that flows off the rear of the egg shape. This will be the shark's lower body.

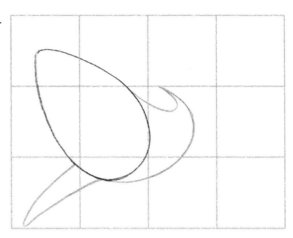

3.

Add the dorsal fin on top of the shark. Be careful to put it in the correct place on the grid. Draw in the four gills near the rear of the egg shape.

Draw the other fin, which goes al- most all the way

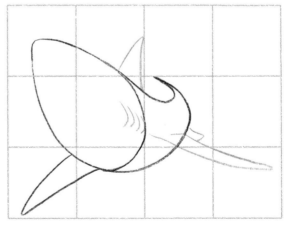

to the right edge of the grid. Add the rear fin behind the right fin.

4.

Draw a curved line from the nose to the top of the first gill. Then draw a small line from the bottom of the last gill to the right fin, and from the right fin around the body. This will separate the colors.

Draw two spots for the nose. Draw in the eye. Put in a shape like an upside down moon for the mouth and add teeth to the top and bottom.

Draw the tall tail and bottom section behind the dorsal fin.

5.

Outline your shark and erase the pencil. You can color your shark grey, dark green or blue.

Sea Horse

Sea horses are fish. They do not have scales but have skin stretched over their bony skeleton. Sea horses are found in the shallow, warmer parts of the ocean. The fin located on their back propels them through the water in a standing position.

1.

Draw a grid with two equal squares going across and four down.

Firstly, draw the oval-shaped head in the top left of the grid. Draw in the body shape, being careful to place it slightly slanted to the right.

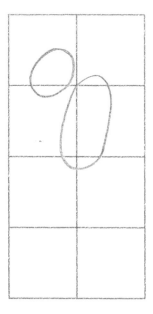

2.

Draw on the snout and neck. Notice how they flow onto the head and body shape. Draw in the twisting tail.

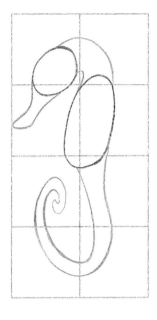

3.

Add the shape on top of the head and the points on the back, running from the top of the neck to the tip of the tail. Draw in the eye and pupil.

Draw slightly curved lines going horizontally across the body of the seahorse from the neck to the end of the tail. These represent the bony skeleton.

Draw a line down the length of the seahorse, curved between each previously drawn horizontal skeletal line. Add another vertical line towards the front of its body.

Draw in the little fin underneath the belly and the large fin on the back.

4.

Outline your drawing and erase the pencil. Sea horses come in many different colors and patterns. You may like to try making up your own color pattern.

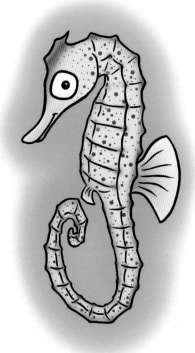

Octopus

The octopus is a master of disguise. It can change its color to mirror its surroundings so it cannot be seen. This camouflage helps it hide from predators. It has great eyesight and can squeeze through very small gaps between rocks to escape.

1.

Draw a grid with four equal squares going across and three down.

Draw a shape for the head in the top right side of the grid. Draw another shape slightly smaller under this for the body.

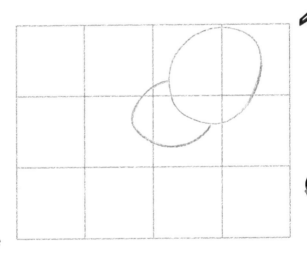

2.

Draw in some curved lines for legs. Be careful to note how and where they fall on the grid.

3.

Draw in the top side of the legs, bringing the tips to a point.

Add the eyes. One of them is outside the head shape and one is inside the head shape. Make the head a little pointier.

4.

Add some suckers to the underside of the legs.

5.

Outline your octopus with your marker and erase the pencil lines. You can color your octopus any color you like as they can mimic every color.

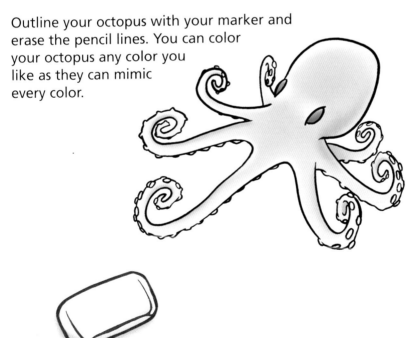

The Crab

Crabs are ten-legged crustaceans that walk sideways. They have two large claws called pincers which they use for feeding or to defend themselves if necessary. All their bones are on the outside. This is called an exoskeleton. There are more than 5000 species of crabs. Some live in the ocean and some live on land.

1.

Draw a grid with four equal squares going across and three down.

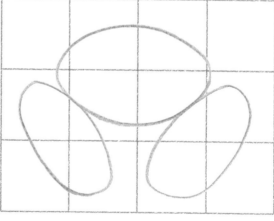

First, draw in an oval for the crab's body. Draw in two more shapes pointing down and towards the center of the grid. These will be the pincers.

2.

Add a shape that is wide at the top and comes to a point for the legs on either side of the body shape.

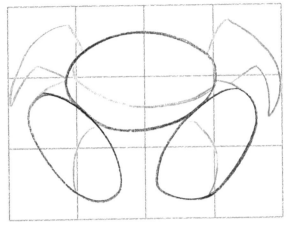

Join the pincer shapes to the body at their tops, below the leg shape we have just drawn.
Draw a curved line on both of the pincers.

Draw a curved line through and just under the middle of the oval for the body.

3.

Break the legs shapes up into three legs using two lines on each.

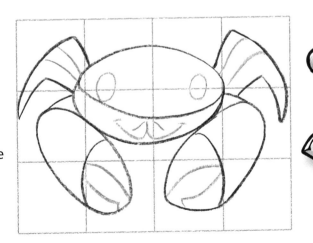

Add the eyes above the middle line in the oval body shape. Draw the mouth parts under this line.

Define the pincers.

4.

Put joints in on the legs. Draw a small hump at the top of the oval for the body shape. Draw in the parts underneath the eye.

Draw in a line to make the bottom of the shell and pincer arms.

5.

Outline your crab with your marker and erase the pencil lines. Color your crab.

Killer Whale

The killer whale is a large marine mammal that hunts for its prey. They hunt in groups and eat fish, squid, seals, penguins and other whales. They have a white underbelly and a white patch behind the eye and near the tail. They can grow to over eight meters long and weigh over three and a half tons. The dorsal fin of a male can reach almost 6 feet (2 meters) tall.

1.

Draw a grid with four equal squares going across and two down.

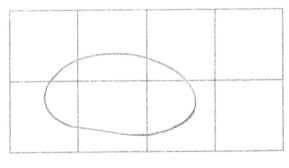

Begin with a shape on the lower part of the grid. This will represent the killer whale's body.

61

2.

Draw the pointy but still rounded nose of the whale, being careful to merge it onto the body shape.

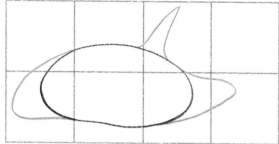

Draw the dorsal fin to the rear of the body shape. Add the shape for the rear of the body.

3.

Draw a little lip on the nose of the whale and continue that line for the mouth. Draw the bottom part of the lip and merge it into the nose.

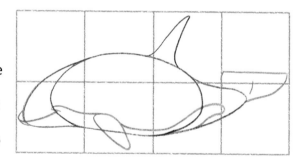

Draw a wavy line through to the rear of the body for the markings. Add the short, stubby flipper. Draw the tail fin shape.

4.

Draw the eye and the marking behind it for the patch of white. Define the tail inside the shape drawn in the last stage.

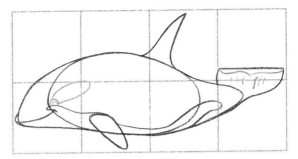

5.

Outline your work and erase the pencil lines. Killer whales are black on top. I have highlighted this to add a three-dimensional look to it. The belly has been shaded with a grey on the underside.

Index